THEN *&* NOW

ORANGE COUNTY

THEN & NOW

ORANGE COUNTY

Chris Epting

This book is dedicated with love to my family: wife Jean, son Charles, daughter Claire, and my mom, Louise. (And Charlie, thank you, son, for helping line so many of these images up—memories I will cherish long after this book has come and gone.)

Copyright © 2011 by Chris Epting
ISBN 978-0-7385-8115-6

Library of Congress Control Number: 2010922856

Published by Arcadia Publishing
Charleston, South Carolina

Printed in the United States of America

For all general information, please contact Arcadia Publishing:
Telephone 843-853-2070
Fax 843-853-0044
E-mail sales@arcadiapublishing.com
For customer service and orders:
Toll-Free 1-888-313-2665

Visit us on the Internet at www.arcadiapublishing.com

ON THE COVER: Seal Beach is pictured around the 1920s. Back then, Seal Beach was like the Coney Island of the West Coast. Nicknamed "Jewel City," it was a playground for stars and tourists alike. Charlie Chaplin, Fatty Arbuckle, Mabel Normand, Mary Pickford, and many other notables visited to enjoy the sand, surf, clubs, bowling alley, plunge, and other attractions. Starting in 1929, as the great depression set in, crowds became sparse and the Sale Beach gradually became a much quieter, tamer place, as it is today. (Photograph courtesy of the Orange County Archives.)

CONTENTS

Acknowledgments		vii
Introduction		ix
1.	North Orange County	11
2.	Central Orange County	27
3.	South Orange County	55
4.	Beach Cities	71

ACKNOWLEDGMENTS

Working on this book has been yet another terrific experience.

Special thanks, as always with a project like this, must go to the exceptional historian Chris Jepsen, assistant archivist at the Orange County Archives, for making so many wonderful historical photographs available and for his great Web site, ochistorical.blogspot.com. Through his efforts, we all become better historians. To the staff at the *Huntington Beach Independent* newspaper, thanks for the support. To Debbie Seracini, Devon E. E. Weston, Kai Oliver-Kurtin, Kate Crawford, and the rest of the Arcadia Publishing staff, thank you for the tireless efforts in helping to document our nation's history.

I'd also like to thank my wife, Jean, for her typical patience and support. To my daughter Claire and son Charlie, I love you immeasurably.

And to each one of you holding this book right now, thank you so much for your interest.

All "then" photographs, unless otherwise noted, are from the author's private collection. All "now" photographs were taken by the author.

INTRODUCTION

Several years ago, on a blistering summer day in New York City, I rushed across town on foot to a location. My destination was the outside of an apartment building. The mission was to take a picture lined up like an old photograph for a then-and-now view of the exact site. After locating the address—and waiting years to shoot in this fashion—I found, to my dismay, that a group of construction workers had chosen the precise site I wanted to shoot as the place to sit and have a leisurely lunch break. This is brought up to illustrate that, no matter how easy it might seem to simply go off and reshoot vintage photographs in their exact original setting, there are many variables that can and, especially if one is short on time, often will pop up to present a challenge. Lighting issues, different lenses from way back that created strange angles and perspectives, traffic (both pedestrian and vehicular) getting in the way, landscaping (both natural and man-made) that has reshaped the terrain, and more. And often these challenges simply add to the fun of doing it.

I have shot then-and-now photographs all over the United States. It's a true passion of mine to stand in the footsteps of another photographer and re-create what he or she framed up decades before. Comparing the two shots is a way to see back in time, to make it a tangible, measurable element—a most exciting proposition. That explains my enthusiasm at the thought of this project—because my family has lived in Orange County for more than a decade, it's our home, and now I can make sense of how history has treated our county and, with this book, can show how time has affected Orange County.

Then-and-now photograph locations usually fall into three basic categories.

First there are the sites that have barely changed at all; and by seeing the comparison, it might be hard to spot any differences. This is good in that it means things have been preserved, but a book full of images that look the same would be boring—exhilarating from a preservationist's point of view (and I am a preservationist at heart) but as a book, dull.

Second are the sites that have changed partially—altered and developed enough so that it's like a game to figure out what is the same and what has changed. Visually these may be the most appealing photographs.

Third are the sites that have changed radically, where today there is an entirely new structure or a vacant lot where the old structures used to stand. These can be the most depressing places to shoot then-and-now photographs. But they are necessary in telling the story.

For this book, all three categories have been blended in order to help present the full spectrum of how things today in Orange County compare to yesteryear. Interestingly, based on my experience in putting this book together, Orange County is divided among those three categories so that almost equal weight can be given to each. Cities like Anaheim and Huntington Beach have seen their downtown areas altered dramatically, yet in Santa Ana, Seal Beach, and Fullerton, much has been preserved. Many old attractions like the Japanese Deer Park and the Alligator Farm are gone, but Disneyland and

Knott's Berry Farm are still going strong. Beaches and parks survive in many cases, but citrus groves are all but a memory. Freeways, as well as toll roads, seem to be taking over the landscape. Time, as you will see in vivid detail, marches on (and the pictures prove it)!

To give a brief history of Orange County, it was formally created as a political entity separate from the county of Los Angeles in 1889. The seemingly endless wilderness had evolved into irrigated farmlands and easy-to-live-in communities supported by a robust, year-round harvest of Valencia oranges, lemons, avocados, walnuts, and more. Agriculture, built upon the labor of many migrant workers, became the primary industry in the new county, and due to the many blossoming orange groves, the region was christened "Orange County."

More and more change was in the air. Huntington Beach became a boomtown with the discovery of oil in the 1920s. In 1926, Pacific Coast Highway opened, connecting Huntington Beach and Newport Beach. The following year, Laguna Beach become incorporated with a population of 1,900. Then San Clemente was incorporated with a population of 650 in 1928 and Doheny Beach State Park opened in 1931 on Capistrano Beach property. In 1943, the El Toro Marine Base opened on 4,000 acres belonging to Irvine Ranch. In 1952, the Los Alamitos race track opened. Buena Park was incorporated with Costa Mesa following the next year. The Santa Ana freeway (I-5) opened in 1954, and in 1955, Walt Disney opened Disneyland in Anaheim. In the late 1950s, aerospace firms and light industry began expanding here, and the increasing population meant more and more jobs at hospitals, restaurants, and stores.

South Orange County began to grow by leaps and bounds in the 1960s with master planned communities such as Irvine, Mission Viejo, and Laguna Niguel. Aliso Viejo, Rancho Santa Margarita, Ladera Ranch, and others followed in the 1980s and 1990s. Today Orange County is home to more than three million residents, with 34 incorporated cities. It is a big, thriving, sprawling place that blends suburbia with the beach and many ethnic enclaves.

We have lots of ground to cover, so with that background, let's head off, shall we? Let's go see how Orange County was back then.

And of course, how it is now.

CHAPTER 1

NORTH ORANGE COUNTY

This image shows the cast of the show *The Streets of New York* from the introductory season of the Bird Cage Theatre at Knott's Berry Farm in 1954. The theater, which still stands but is only used sporadically, was created as a replica of the historic Bird Cage Theatre in Tombstone, Arizona. (Then photograph courtesy of the Orange County Archives.)

In the 1920s, Walter Knott sold berries and pies with his family from a roadside stand on Highway 39 (today Beach Boulevard) in Buena Park. In 1934, to make ends meet, Knott's wife, Cordelia, starting serving her soon-to-be-famous fried chicken to hungry travelers. As time progressed, attractions were put in to accommodate the guests who waited for a seat at the chicken dinner restaurant. Those attractions were the beginning of the popular Knott's Berry Farm amusement park. Today coasters tower over the site of the original restaurant, which has been incorporated into an expanded structure. (Then photograph courtesy of the Orange County Archives.)

THE SLIDE

California
Alligator Farm

This is the old California Alligator Farm as it looked in 1955. It started as the Los Angeles Alligator Farm, next door to the Los Angeles Ostrich Farm in Lincoln Heights, and was a wildly popular tourist attraction from 1907 to 1953. Then it moved to Buena Park and was renamed the California Alligator Farm and also featured snakes, tortoises, and other reptiles. The attraction remained there until 1984, at which point it closed and the critters were shipped to a private estate in Florida. Today the Beach Boulevard location is a Claim Jumper restaurant and this adjacent open field.

On October 31, 1924, Babe Ruth and Walter Johnson played a barnstorming game here that became a solid part of the area's folklore. Sponsored by the Anaheim Elks Club, it was a homecoming for Johnson of sorts, in that he grew up in the neighboring oil town of Olinda. Nearly 5,000 people turned out for the event at the Brea Bowl field to see Ruth's team win, 12–1. Today the Brea Bowl site is a residential neighborhood, though the natural "bowl" of the area is still intact.

The Japanese Gardens and Deer Park opened in Buena Park in the 1960s and lasted until the mid-1970s. It featured Japanese pearl divers, cultural Japanese shows, many deer roaming the property, koi ponds, and many more elements relating to Japanese culture. Several years before closing, it morphed into the Enchanted Village theme park, thanks to new ownership. Today the site, located off Knott Avenue, is a corporate park and no trace of the attraction remains.

This is near the intersection of Jacaranda Place and Highland Avenue, a charming residential street in Fullerton. The then image shows the area in 1938, and today the houses and even the old-fashioned streetlamps remain just as they did back then, a rarity in Orange County, where many residential streets have been redeveloped. (Then photograph courtesy of the Orange County Archives.)

The famed Knott's Berry Farm Chicken Dinner restaurant is shown as it looked in 1965. Today, while the physical structure of the restaurant has not changed, the environment around the restaurant has, as roller coasters loom overhead. The restaurant now seats more than 900 guests at a time, serves more than one-and-a-half million guests each year, and is the largest full-service restaurant in California that serves chicken as its main course. (Then photograph courtesy of the Orange County Archives.)

This is 100 East Central Avenue in La Habra as it looked in 1965 and how it looks today. Back then it was a local pharmacy, and today it is the site of an office building. And the location plays an important part in La Habra history. This is the original site of the town of La Habra's store and post office. La Habra was founded in 1896. The site is now marked with a plaque, which contains the bell of the first Catholic church in the area. (Then photograph courtesy of the Orange County Archives.)

Located at 301 South Euclid Street in La Habra, the former Union Pacific depot, seen here in 1965, now serves as the Children's Museum of La Habra—the first Children's Museum west of the Rocky Mountains. (It opened in 1977.) The building dates back to 1923 and is a very popular place for both locals and visitors from out of town. (Then photograph courtesy of the Orange County Archives.)

Located next to the La Habra Children's Museum is the former La Habra Pacific Electric Depot, the site of the earliest railroad line in the La Habra area. The depot building was moved from its original site across the street and has been refurbished. Today it is used as a community theater and is a vibrant part of the La Habra community. (Then photograph courtesy of the Orange County Archives.)

These images depict Main Street in 1930 Yorba Linda and today. The large building in the center of both shots is the Yorba Linda Masonic Hall. Originally erected in 1913 as a community center, the building was also home to the first drugstore in the town. The building was rededicated by the grand master of Masons in California on August 23, 1986, and a new symbolic cornerstone was laid in the northeast corner of the building. A time capsule was placed behind it with instructions to retrieve its contents in 50 years.

The Model Food Market in the Sunny Hills community (part of Fullerton) stood at 125 Valencia Mesa Drive and is pictured in 1961. Today the site has been completely redeveloped and is now home to St. Jude Medical Center. (Then photograph courtesy of the Orange County Archives.)

The Movieland Wax museum, one of the largest of its kind in the world, was located at 7711 Beach Boulevard in Buena Park. After being open for 43 years and serving over 10 million visitors, it closed on October 31, 2005. About 50 of the museum's celebrity figures were shipped to a sister museum in San Francisco, and 80 others went to a museum in South Korea. Most of the rest were put up for public auction in March 2006, which brought in over $1 million. Today the building still stands, and the celebrity handprints are still on the ground in cement in front of the structure. (Then photograph courtesy of the Orange County Archives.)

The Yorba Cemetery in Placentia is shown as it looked in 1969 and how it appears today. The history of the cemetery dates all the way back to 1834, when Don Bernardo Yorba petitioned Mexican governor José Figueroa for 13,000 acres of land on the northern side of the banks of the Santa Ana River. In 1858, Bernardo deeded a plot of land a quarter mile west of his adobe ranch house to the bishop of the Catholic church. It became the oldest private cemetery in Orange County, predated only by the mission cemetery in San Juan Capistrano. The cemetery was closed in 1939 but was reopened in the late 1960s. The large grave in the center of both photographs is that of Bernardo Yorba. (Then photograph courtesy of the Orange County Archives.)

This is the marker for California State Historical Landmark No. 226, the Don Bernardo Yorba Ranch House site. According to the California State Parks Office of Historic Preservation, "Here Don Bernardo Yorba created the greatest rancho of California's Golden Age, combining the Santa Ana Grant awarded to his father by the King of Spain in 1810 and lands granted to him by Governor José Figueroa in 1834. He was the third son of José Antonio Yorba, who came with Don Gaspar de Portolá in 1769 to establish California's first family." The then photograph dates back to 1961. The area around the marker has since been developed into a residential neighborhood. (Then photograph courtesy of the Orange County Archives.)

These images are looking north on Main Street in Yorba Linda in 1920 and today. At the time of the then image, the population of Yorba Linda was only 350 and Richard Nixon, who was born here, would have been about seven years old. Five years earlier, Troop No. 99, the first Boy Scout troop in Orange County, was organized in Yorba Linda. Today it is easy to see how the mountains line up, but the original post office (which opened in 1912), the dry goods store, and the restaurant are all long gone. (Then photograph courtesy of the Orange County Archives.)

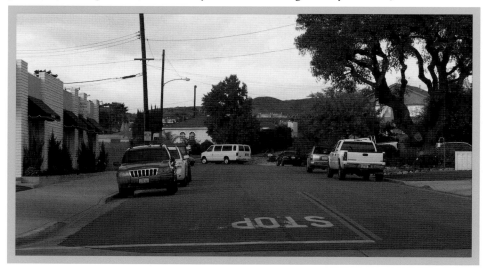

CHAPTER 2

CENTRAL
ORANGE COUNTY

LEMON HEIGHTS Orange Co. Cal.

Shown here is a citrus ranch in Lemon Heights owned by C. E. Utt and Sherman Stevens. The location was just northeast of Tustin, and the date of this image is 1910. A large amount of trees are visible, with rolling hills in the background.

Today the commercial citrus industry has all but vanished from Orange County, replaced instead with various other industries. (Then photograph courtesy of the Orange County Archives.)

This is historic Plaza Square in the city of Orange, looking down South Glassell Street around 1920 in the then image. The Huff Jeweler building, at right, still stands (as many of the other buildings do in this historic district). The upper level of the building is now a law firm and the ground floor is an Italian restaurant. In addition to the historic preservation, Plaza Square is also well known (and popular) for its many diverse antique shops and interesting restaurants.

The then image shows Anaheim Stadium as it looked during its opening week in April 1966. The iconic "Big A" can be seen beyond the left wall, where it sat until the stadium's first renovation in 1979, when it was moved to the edge of the parking lot. Today the stadium has been completely redesigned and the surrounding area has been greatly developed. Just beyond center field is the arena where the Anaheim Ducks hockey team plays today.

The *c.* 1960 image shows the intersection of Walker Street and North Vonnie Lane in Cypress. Most of the original houses remain, though the grocery store on the right has been updated today into a mini mall. Cypress was originally called Waterville due to the many wells in the area, but it then became Dairy City. In 1957, residents voted on the name Cypress as an homage to the Cypress Elementary School, built in 1895, which adopted the name from the Cypress trees planted to buffer the schoolhouse from the Santa Ana winds. (Then photograph courtesy of the Orange County Archives.)

The then image shows South Glassell Street looking north toward Plaza Square, in Old Towne Orange, around 1909. South Glassell is still unpaved in the then shot, and streetcar tracks can be seen down the center, with a trolley car visible in the background at the plaza. At the far right is the first location for Dittmer's Mission Pharmacy (131 South Glassell Street). On the north side of it are Peterkin's Restaurant (127 South Glassell Street) and Orange City Garage (123 South Glassell Street). Today several of the structures remain.

Peters Canyon Reservoir in Tustin is seen in 1966 and today. This park was part of the original Spanish land grant Rancho Lomas de Santiago. In 1899, a group of sportsmen introduced the game of golf into Orange County, creating a nine-hole course right near this site. During World War II, Peters Canyon was used as a training area for the U.S. Army, and today it is a beautiful park run by the County of Orange. (Then photograph courtesy of the Orange County Archives.)

In the then image, we see the H. Clay Kellogg House as it looked at its original location in Santa Ana in 1903. It was designed by Hiram (H. Clay) Kellogg, a native Californian and one of Orange County's pioneers. The house was originally located in downtown Santa Ana at 122 Orange Street, but it was moved to the grounds of the Heritage Museum of Orange County in Santa Ana in 1980. Today it is used for hands-on education about the Victorian era for more than 18,000 children each year.

The old Del Campo Hotel, located at the northeast corner of Broadway and South Olive Street in Anaheim, was built in 1888. It was owned by A. H. Denker of Los Angeles and built by the Albrecht brothers. The building also housed the first osteopathic college in California, the Pacific Sanitarium and School of Osteopathy. In 1905, the hotel was sold and torn down. The lumber was sold for $6,000. The then image shows a corner view looking east along Olive towards Broadway, with the hotel's main entrance on the right. A sign visible on the balcony at left side says "Del Campo." Today the site is a park.

This is Lemon Street in Anaheim, looking north across West Center Street. The then image shows the Henry Brothers Drug Store on the northwest corner, with Roberts Apartments above, and A. E. Howard Auto Repair. On the opposite side of the street are Cecil Rooms (in the right foreground), H. A. Nelson Optometrist, and Platt's Snooker Parlor. A bank has replaced the drugstore, and a mall has replaced almost everything else.

This view looks west on Lincoln Avenue (formerly Center Street) in Anaheim from Los Angeles Street (now Anaheim Boulevard). The then shot was taken in February 1962. Clearly the redevelopment of the 1970s and 1980s gave the downtown Anaheim area a complete facelift. Virtually nothing remains from the older photograph.

Downtown Anaheim is shown as it looked in 1961 and how it looks today. In the then image is the SQR store (left) located at 202 West Lincoln Avenue (formerly West Center Street). It was established in 1907 by August Schumacher, Wesley Quarton, and Oscar Renner, hence the initials. The building was constructed in 1925 and demolished in 1978 during Redevelopment Project Alpha. Today an office building takes up most of the site.

The view shows downtown Santa Ana looking east on Fourth Street in 1956. In the distance are the Santa Ana Mountains, the landmark clock is visible on the Spurgeon building on the right, and just beyond that, the American flag can be seen on top of the First National Bank. Past that, several signs are visible, including Steele's and Cover Girl Sports Wear. Today, as one can easily compare, many of the original buildings remain, though the businesses have changed.

This is Santa Ana City Hall, located at the corner of Third and Main Streets in Santa Ana. It was built in 1935, and this particular city hall replaced one that had been constructed on the same corner in 1904 and was severely damaged in the 1933 Long Beach earthquake. Today little has changed, as the building has been completely preserved since 1935.

This is the Orange County Courthouse at 211 West Santa Ana Boulevard. It is the oldest existing county courthouse in Southern California, built in 1900 of hand-hewn Arizona red sandstone. During Santa Ana's Centennial (1969–1970) it was registered as California State Historical Landmark No. 837. The March 1933 Long Beach earthquake (a 6.4 shaker) resulted in the tower being taken down. In the then image, debris from the quake is visible on the steps.

At far left in both images is the Otis building at the corner of Fourth and Main Streets in Santa Ana. It was built in 1925. At right in the then image, taken in 1954, is the Montgomery Ward building on the corner of East Fourth and North Main Streets, which was torn down in 1975. Today a bank occupies the site.

The Warner Avenue Bridge dedication took place on June 29, 1961. Pictured next to the marker is Supt. Willis Warner. Warner was a prominent Orange County government official who served on the Orange County Board of Supervisors from 1939 to 1963 and was its chairman for almost 15 years. He was known for his extensive work on flood control and sanitation issues. Warner Avenue, formerly Wintersburg Avenue, was renamed for Willis Warner in the 1960s. Today the bridge has been widened and the plaque no longer remains.

CENTRAL ORANGE COUNTY

This view looks north up Knott Avenue from about Orangewood Avenue on the border between Garden Grove and Cypress, near Stanton. In the distance of the c. 1962 shot, a spherical radar station is visible in the background. It complimented a Nike Missile emplacement. Today Knott has been widened and the area has been dramatically developed.

Here is the Orco Block Company on Beach Boulevard near Katella Avenue in Stanton. Orco is a leading manufacturer of concrete masonry units, specialty mortars, and paving stones and has been for more than 60 years. The then shot dates back to 1955. Today the actual plant is not visible, but we can see the Orco Block office building at right on Beach Boulevard. (Then photograph courtesy of the Orange County Archives.)

Katella Avenue at Reagan Street in Los Alamitos is pictured around 1955 and today. The church at right has been replaced with another church, and most of the trees have been replaced by widened streets and general urban development, as has much of this part of Orange County. (Then photograph courtesy of the Orange County Archives.)

This is Newport Boulevard at Eighteenth Street in Costa Mesa around 1963 and today. Most of the smaller businesses have been replaced with newer businesses, though the area still remains a bustling commercial hub of the area. Historically, Costa Mesa surged in population during and after World War II as thousand of soldiers trained at nearby Santa Ana Army Air Base and then returned to the city after the war with their families. (Then photograph courtesy of the Orange County Archives.)

This is Harbor Boulevard at Heil Avenue in Fountain Valley. The then photograph, taken in the early 1960s, shows the Brookhurst Dairy and other businesses on the right. The dairy was in business for several years in the 1960s. Today Mile Square Park is located beyond where the dairy was, and the traffic light we see in the now shot is Heil Avenue, which was named for local farmer Vernon C. Heil. (Then photograph courtesy of the Orange County Archives.)

This view shows Bolsa Avenue and Jackson Street in Midway City in the 1960s and today. Midway City is an unincorporated community bordered by Westminster to its east and Huntington Beach to its west. It got its name because it is located midway between Long Beach and Santa Ana It is one of Orange County's oldest communities, and many of its homes are 1950s construction. (Midway City is also where actress Michelle Pfeiffer hails from.) The market building on the right remains virtually unchanged in the now image. (Then photograph courtesy of the Orange County Archives.)

The old Barber City Woman's Club building, which still stands at 14046 Rancho Road, was also used for a time as a branch of the Orange County Public Library. The then image dates back to the 1950s. The community of Barber City is now part of the city of Westminster. (Then photograph courtesy of the Orange County Archives.)

August 11, 1955, was a big day in Anaheim: the Nixon family visited Disneyland. In the crowd outside Disneyland City Hall are Vice Pres. Richard M. Nixon, First Lady Patricia Nixon, daughters Tricia Nixon and Julie Nixon, actor Fess Parker, and assorted other friends and fans. Today the building at the famed theme park remains essentially the same.

Another monumental day at Disneyland, November 23, 1958, saw a real-life princess visit the park. From left to right in the then photograph at the park's entrance are heiress Mme. Mary Carolou; Princess Sophia of Greece; and their special hostess for the day, actress (and Mouseketeer) Annette Funicello. In the now shot, the author's family poses in place of the three women.

In the then image, construction of Disneyland's Sleeping Beauty Castle is underway in 1955, with a cement walkway already formed in the left foreground. Ladders and piles of supplies sit around the frame of the forming castle and workers stand high around the top of the castle's towers. Today, of course, we see the finished product, the venerable icon of Disneyland in all of its glory.

The Hotel Valencia in downtown Anaheim was located on the corner of 182 West Center Street (now Lincoln Avenue) and Lemon Street. It was built in 1916 by John Ziegler for $40,000 and designed by architect M. Eugene Durfee on the exact same site as two previous hotels, the Anaheim Hotel and the Commercial Hotel. The Hotel Valencia was destroyed by a fire in 1977 and today an office building occupies the site. This part of Anaheim has been dramatically redeveloped in the last several decades, removing essentially all traces of the past, at least along Lincoln Avenue.

Here is one last view of
downtown Anaheim.
In the 1961 then image,
Center Street is viewed
from the corner of
Lemon Street, with the
old SQR department
store on the left. Down
Center Street on the
right is the old Fox
Theater, with a view
of old Mother Colony
restaurant as well.
Today literally every old
structure is gone, razed
in the 1970s–1980s
redevelopment of
downtown Anaheim.

CHAPTER

SOUTH ORANGE
COUNTY

This is the El Camino motor service station in San Clemente around 1920. Notice how all of the motorists are posing for the photograph. The station is no longer there.

This is the intersection of Browning Avenue and Irvine Boulevard in Tustin, both today and around 1960. The city of Tustin was established as a real estate venture by a Petaluma carriage maker named Columbus Tustin. He and his partner, Nelson O. Stafford, bought about 1,300 acres of the Rancho Santiago de Santa Ana in 1868 when the old Spanish land grant was being partitioned. In the now image, it is easy to see how the area has become more developed since 1960. (Then photograph courtesy of the Orange County Archives.)

In the then image, we see downtown San Juan Capistrano in 1962, looking just about two blocks west from the entrance of the historic Mission San Juan Capistrano. The building on the right was the old Capistrano Hotel, which would be demolished for a shopping project the following year. Today San Juan Capistrano features a blend of historic buildings and newer structures. Along with the famed swallows that visit the city, the mission is still an extremely popular draw for both tourists and locals.

Here we see Crown Valley Parkway at Forbes Road in Laguna Niguel in 1976 and today. Laguna Niguel was one of the first master planned communities in California. Originally conceived in the early 1960s, Laguna Niguel became incorporated in 1989 as Orange County's 29th city. In the modern image, you can see the development at the crest of the hill, and a gas station still remains on the right hand corner. (Then photograph courtesy of the Orange County Archives.)

The Tustin Marine Corps Air Station (seen here in the then image in 1968) was established in 1942 as Santa Ana Naval Air Station, a base for airship operations in support of the U.S. Navy's coastal patrol efforts during World War II. NAS Santa Ana was decommissioned in 1949. In 1951, the facility was reactivated to support the Korean War. It was the country's first air facility developed solely for helicopter operations. The base ceased operations in 1999, and plans for the famous blimp hangars remain up in the air. Both buildings were designated National Civil Engineering Landmarks by the American Society of Civil Engineers.

These images show El Toro Road Lake Forest in 1970 and today. In just 40 years, the area has become incredibly developed and the rustic view toward the mountains has been clearly altered. Lake Forest, currently the most densely populated city in South Orange County, was only incorporated as a city in December 1991. Since being incorporated, it has expanded its limits to include the communities of Foothill Ranch and Portola Hills. (Then photograph courtesy of the Orange County Archives.)

El Toro Road and Paseo de Valencia in Laguna Woods are pictured around 1965 and today. Laguna Woods was only incorporated in 1999 as Orange County's 32nd city. Interestingly, the average age of Laguna Woods's residents is 78. That is because 90 percent of the city's 4 square miles is contained within the gated senior citizen community of Laguna Woods Village (formerly Leisure World, Laguna Hills). (Then photograph courtesy of the Orange County Archives.)

This is Rancho Viejo Road, looking south, in San Juan Capistrano, around 1964 and today. What had once been wide open hills and fields for agriculture and cattle has given way to residences, golf courses, parks, schools, and other developments as the area's population exploded in the last 40 years or so. Interstate 5 can still be seen to the right. (Then photograph courtesy of the Orange County Archives.)

Paseo de Valencia at Alicia Parkway in Laguna Hills is pictured in 1978 and today. As is the case with much of south Orange County, the area has undergone intense development in the last 20–30 years. The city of Laguna Hills was incorporated in 1991 and first gained recognition when the private senior community Leisure World was developed. The community of Leisure World has now incorporated into the city of Laguna Woods.

Canyon Grocery was located at 22178 Laguna Canyon Road, at the corner of Woodland Drive in Laguna Beach. At first glance, it appears nothing is left from the 1957 image, the wooden clapboard house at the right still stands (and it seems a flood channel has been dug at the exact site where the store once stood). (Then photograph courtesy of the Orange County Archives.)

Lion Country Safari was located in Irvine from 1970 to 1984. An interesting event occurred here when an aging circus lion from Mexico was given to the facility. One day, he sired a litter of cubs, the result of having several lionesses that were attracted to the lazy lion. His name was Frasier the Sensuous Lion, and he became the rage, drawing huge visitors to the site. In 1973, Lion Country tried to capitalize on their new star. A movie was made called *Frasier the Sensuous Lion*. T-shirts, watches, and other souvenirs were sold featuring Frasier until 1974, when he died and was buried on the grounds. Today a water park and amphitheater take up most of the property, but some of the abandoned roads where animals roamed can still be found, as seen in the now image.

Avery and Marguerite Parkways in Mission Viejo are pictured here in 1976 and today. As is the case with much of south Orange County, a good deal of development has taken place in the last few decades. Mission Viejo is considered one of the largest master planned communities ever built under a single project in the United States and is rivaled only by Highlands Ranch, Colorado, in its size. The city's name is a reference to Rancho Mission Viejo, a large Spanish land grant from which the community was founded. There is no Spanish mission in Mission Viejo, and the name is an improper use of a masculine adjective with a feminine noun. The correct Spanish term meaning "old mission" is *misión vieja*.

A horse waits on the curb on the side of the Capistrano Market, once located on Verdugo Street in San Juan Capistrano, around 1960. Today a shopping plaza is located on the site. The famed Mission San Juan Capistrano was established by Franciscan missionaries in 1776. The city itself was officially incorporated in 1961. (Then photograph courtesy of the Orange County Archives.)

Red Hill Avenue at San Juan Street in Tustin is shown in 1965 and today. Interstate 5 is still visible at center left, but the area has been dramatically redeveloped in the nearly 50 years that separate each image. The church on the right is gone and a fast food restaurant can now be seen at left. (Then photograph courtesy of the Orange County Archives.)

SOUTH ORANGE COUNTY

Camp Myford was located near Little Peters Lake in Tustin from 1952 to 1988. The site was maintained by the Boy Scouts for many weekend scouting events and more than 20 years of day camp during the summer for Cub Scouts. It was named for James Irvine's youngest son, Myford Irvine, as the property had been a gift from The Irvine Company. Today a gated community, Tustin Ranch Estates, occupies the site where Camp Myford used to be.

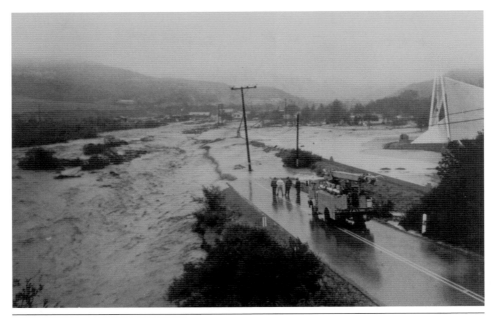

The then image shows the 1969 flood that destroyed Silverado Canyon Road flowing in front of the Silverado Canyon Community Church. A truck and four people are standing on the road, looking at the damaged area. A similarly devastating storm, in 1939, also washed away bridges and roads. Founded all the way back in 1878, Silverado Canyon is located in the Santa Ana Mountains. As is visible in the now image, the church remains and the road has been fully repaired. Interestingly, ancient sea life fossils can be found within the sandstone cliffs in this area. Millions of years ago, the area was under the ocean.

CHAPTER 4

BEACH CITIES

Dana Point Harbor, 1957

Dana Point was named for Richard Henry Dana Jr., author of *Two Years Before the Mast*, which included a description of the area. He referred to Stillwater Bay (now Capistrano Bay) as the "most romantic spot on the Coast." This 1957 postcard shows some development in the harbor area where today there is an ocean research center and a replica of *The Pilgrim*, the 1830 schooner that Dana sailed.

71

The famed Golden Bear Café opened in 1929 at what is today 306 Pacific Coast Highway. It can be seen here on the left in the then photograph, taken in the early 1930s near the intersection of Main Street and Ocean Avenue. A bit of the metal archway that used to greet visitors in the 1930s is visible in the upper right of the photograph. The Golden Bear was razed in the mid-1980s.

The Huntington Beach Post Office at 316 Olive Street was a Works Progress Administration (WPA) project that opened in 1935. In the then photograph, the building is seen several months before the big grand opening event that took place and many finishing touches have yet to be added.

Today the building retains all of its architectural integrity and is one of the last historic structures left on Main Street. It has a sister building in Santa Paula, California, another post office built from the same blueprints.

From Pacific Avenue in Sunset Beach, one gets a good view of one of the most unique residences in Orange County. The Water Tower House located at 1 Anderson Street is a luxury tri-level home with two master suites, bar, fire pit lounge, outdoor Jacuzzi, and office in a view room at the top. In 1945, water was pumped from an artesian well from Bolsa Chica bluffs to the tower to service Sunset Beach and Surfside. The tower was deactivated in 1974. By 1985, it had been converted into a house. The then image dates back to 1966.

The Bolsa Chica Gun Club in Huntington Beach opened in the 1890s, when well-to-do Los Angeles businessmen migrated to Orange County and began establishing duck hunting clubs, or gun clubs, throughout the area. Hunters traveled from around the globe to shoot ducks, geese, pelicans, and other species found throughout the ponds and swamps in this area close to the coast. In the 1933 then image, the club can be seen in the upper portion of the photograph. Inspectors are checking for damage the day after the 1933 Long Beach earthquake. Today the palm trees mark the ruins of the long-gone club. The building was razed in the 1970s.

The Golden Bear opened at 306 Pacific Coast Highway as a Huntington Beach restaurant in the 1920s. By the early 1960s, the space had morphed into a music club. The Doors, Dizzy Gillespie, the Byrds, Janis Joplin, and many others played the Bear. Junior Wells cut a live album at the Bear. Peter Tork was a dishwasher there just before being cast as a Monkee. In the 1970s, Linda Ronstadt, Steve Martin, Blondie, the Ramones, Neil Young, and dozens of other major celebrities played the Bear. Guitarist Robin Trower played the last show there on January 26, 1986, and several months later the club was demolished. Today retail space occupies the site.

For more than 100 years, the Huntington Beach Fourth of July parade has entertained millions of people. Here a portion of the parade passes along Walnut Street in 1951, past the Helme House on the right and the Helme Furniture Building in the center. Today all of the buildings in the then image remain, no small feat in a city that has undergone dramatic development in the last two decades.

The original caption slip on this February 1952 then image of Seal Beach reads as follows: "Double rows of sand barricade beach apartment houses from threatening sea. Beach is getting narrower year by year from erosion. Boy pictured is James W. Alexander, 9, walking on sand." Today on Seal Beach, despite the erosion claims being made in 1952, it seems as if the beach has actually gotten a lot wider!

It started out as the Airport Club in the 1920s but became best know as the Glide'er Inn, located at 1400 Pacific Coast Highway in Seal Beach, originally adjacent to a local landing strip and airport. Charles Lindberg, Amelia Earhart, and other famed aviators ate here and signed a logbook that, for years, was on display at the front of the restaurant. Today it is called Mahe, but that plane suspended from the roof hints at the building's former history.

Here we see the Balboa Pavilion around 1910 in the then image. In it, there are two people strolling in front of a row of 10 identical bathhouse cottages on the right side of the image while the train station is in the background. A sign on the two-story station reads "Balboa Beach." The station itself has a covered porch and balcony, as well as a cupola. There is an electric rail car on the left side of the image. Today the pavilion remains, but the quaint beach city has been somewhat developed since 1910.

This is the Balboa Island Ferry in 1948 and today. In 1919, Joseph Alen Beek obtained the rights from the City of Newport Beach to provide a ferry service across the Newport Harbor between Balboa Island and the Balboa Peninsula. Back then, he charged a nickel per person. The family still owns and operates the ferry, and the charge is $1 per adult, $2 per vehicle, 50¢ for children ages 5–11, $1.25 for adults on bikes, 75¢ for children on bikes, $1.50 for motorcycles, and children under the age of five are free. In the background of both images, the Balboa Pavilion and Fun Zone amusement park can be seen, left and right, respectively.

The Buffalo Ranch was a Newport tourist attraction that opened in 1955. Families could drive around the ranch and watch buffalo graze, then visit an Indian village and even eat buffalo burgers. By the 1970s, the place had closed and most of the remaining buffalo had been shipped off to private owners. Today at the site on MacArthur Boulevard (near Bison Avenue, named in honor of the attraction) a buffalo statue and plaque pay homage to what used to be here. (Then photograph courtesy of the Orange County Archives.)

The China House (center of the 1956 then image) was built in Corona Del Mar in 1929 by Pasadena residents W. J. and Sara Lindsay. Due to its ornate curled horns, lacquered bridges, and ornate gold-leaf dragons, it quickly became the inspiration for which the China Cove neighborhood is named. It was torn down in 1986, but a piece of the roof remains a block away, built into another house. On the right in the now image, the empty foundation from the older image can be seen, but it has been built upon.

Looking inland down Goldenwest Street from Pacific Coast Highway in the *c.* 1940s image below, the oil boom was about 20 years old in Huntington Beach, and the city had become a virtual forest of oil derricks in certain areas. Today, though there are still a few active wells, for the most part the structures have been replaced with homes.

For more than a century, the Dory Fleet's fish market near Newport Pier has been a popular local source for fresh seafood. Founded in 1891, the day's catch is sold out of weather-beaten boats that function as sales counters and table tops where fish are beheaded and cleaned before customers' eyes. Here in the then image, we see the Dory Fleet in 1960. Today, looking across the way, it is easy to see many of the older building remain. (Then photograph courtesy of the Orange County Archives.)

Sam's Seafood in Sunset Beach, a 40,000-square-foot tiki bar and restaurant, opened back in the 1920s (as Sam's Sea Foods). It was closed in July 2006 and was slated to get knocked down, but it has since reopened as another restaurant, with the original structure fully intact. The then image is actually a vintage postcard (and the original location was about a mile away from the site where the restaurant is today).

The Seal Beach Naval Weapons Station is also home to the West Coast site of the World War II Submarine Memorial. Commissioned in 1944, the station became fully functional in the early 1950s to accommodate the navy for the Korean War. The station also maintains the Seal Beach National Wildlife Refuge on its property. The then image dates back to the 1950s.

First constructed as McFadden Wharf in 1888, Newport Pier is one of several prominent piers in Newport Beach. From this wooden structure, one can look south to see the Balboa Pier, the second major pier in Newport. This is where the dory fishermen dock their dory boats and bring in their catch of the day, selling it to the public. As evident in the then image from 1960 and the modern image, refreshingly little has changed here. (Then photograph courtesy of the Orange County Archives.)

This is the strand at Newport Beach in 1905 and today. It was in this year that the Pacific Electric Railroad reached Newport, connecting the city by rail with Los Angeles and thus beginning its rapid transit service. The next year, the Pacific Electric rails extended to Balboa and Newport Beach became incorporated as a city.

Laguna Beach is the second-oldest city in Orange County, behind San Juan Capistrano. It is famous for having some of the most beautiful beaches in southern California. It is also renowned for its hotels, shopping, restaurants, world-famous art galleries, and art festivals. In the then image, protesters march as part of a freedom demonstration taking place along Pacific Coast Highway in 1962. The historic White House restaurant, still in business today as a nightclub, can be seen at right.

These shots depict a view looking from the pier up Main Street. The then photograph, which dates to the early 1920s, gives a good idea of how fast Huntington Beach grew once oil was discovered. The building marked "Furniture" on the left is the only structure that remains today (though it is overshadowed by modern buildings in the now photograph).

Seal Beach in the 1920s was like the Coney Island of the West Coast. Nicknamed "Jewel City," it was a playground for stars and tourists alike. Charlie Chaplin, Fatty Arbuckle, Mabel Normand, Mary Pickford, and many other notables visited to enjoy the sand, surf, clubs, bowling alley, plunge, and other attractions. Staring in 1929, as the Great Depression set in, crowds became sparse and Seal Beach gradually became a much quieter, tamer place, as it is today. This view from the pier illustrates how much things changed. It is hard to believe there was once an amusement park right there. (Then photograph courtesy of the Orange County Archives.)

The church building at 401 Sixth Street was dedicated in 1906, three years before Huntington Beach was incorporated. This is the oldest church building still standing in this city. In 1972, the building was purchased by a small group of faithful believers who then turned it into the Community Bible Church, which is what it is today. The then photograph was taken in 1906, and one can see in the recent shot that, while the area around the church has been filled in, the church itself remains much the same.

Matthew E. Helme, a member of the first board of trustees in Huntington Beach, also served as its fourth mayor. He owned the first furniture store, and the original building still stands and is owned and operated by family members today.

Thankfully, the building looks much as it did 100 years ago, which is when the then photograph was taken. Today a car sits where the horse once stood, and a more modern version of the old bike sits in the window.

Heading east along Ocean Avenue (today called Pacific Coast Highway) toward downtown Huntington Beach is still an exhilarating drive. In the then shot, however, taken in the 1930s, the smell of oil would have fought with the salty air. (The beach is just off to the right.) Today, though some oil is still being brought up in the area, it is nothing like it was back then, when a forest of towers ran up and down the coast. This is a final example of an ever-changing Orange County landscape—a place hopefully someone else will choose to compare photographs of in another 50 years or so.

www.arcadiapublishing.com

MAP SEARCH

Discover books about the town where you grew up, the cities where your friends and families live, the town where your parents met, or even that retirement spot you've been dreaming about. Our Web site provides history lovers with exclusive deals, advanced notification about new titles, e-mail alerts of author events, and much more.

MADE IN THE USA

Arcadia Publishing, the leading local history publisher in the United States, is committed to making history accessible and meaningful through publishing books that celebrate and preserve the heritage of America's people and places. Consistent with our mission to preserve history on a local level, this book was printed in South Carolina on American-made paper and manufactured entirely in the United States.

This book carries the accredited Forest Stewardship Council (FSC) label and is printed on 100 percent FSC-certified paper. Products carrying the FSC label are independently certified to assure consumers that they come from forests that are managed to meet the social, economic, and ecological needs of present and future generations.

FSC

Mixed Sources
Product group from well-managed forests and other controlled sources

Cert no. SW-COC-001530
www.fsc.org
© 1996 Forest Stewardship Council

Find *Your* Place in History.